CHINESE RUGS DESIGNED FOR NEEDLEPOINT

Also by Maggie Lane

Needlepoint by Design

More Needlepoint by Design

CHINESE RUGS DESIGNED FOR NEEDLEPOINT

Maggie Lane

Photography by R. Lans Christensen

Charles Scribner's Sons   **New York**

Library of Congress Cataloging in Publication Data

Lane, Maggie.
    Chinese rugs designed for needlepoint.

    Bibliography: p.111

    1. Canvas embroidery. 2. Rugs, Chinese.
I. Title.
TT778.C3L28   746.7'4   75-5733
ISBN 0-684-14195-7

5 7 9 11 13 15 17 19 C/MD 20 18 16 14 12 10 8 6

Printed in the United States of America

TO

Charles Blackburn

Barbara Rubinstein

Lois Cowles

Louise de Paoli

Paul Griffith

Candy McCandliss

Robert G. Taylor

Acknowledgements

My most grateful thanks goes to each one of the people to whom this book is dedicated. Their enthusiasm and their many hours of labor made possible the collection of finished rugs contained in this volume.

To Miss Jean Mailey, Assistant Curator of the Textile Study Room at the Metropolitan Museum of Art, I extend my thanks for introducing me to the embroidered elephant hanging which inspired the panel appearing on the jacket of this book.

To Rosetta Larsen and the members of her establishment (which, alas, closed its doors this past summer), I wish to express the deepest gratitude for their courtesy to me, and for the careful way in which they blocked, backed and bound each rug in the collection even while totally involved in the process of winding up their business affairs.

To Miss Ann Greenberg I wish to express my appreciation for her kindness in lending me so many of her valuable books on Oriental rugs.

And to Elinor Parker I want to give thanks for her help in editing this book.

Preface

One day last summer I sat with a friend in the garden behind her house. After a time she withdrew to shadowed rooms to make tall, iced drinks for us to sip as we talked. While she was gone I lay back in the chaise, listened to the muffled roar of New York traffic, then looked up at the sky. Tall buildings around the walled-in court cut off all but a narrow patch directly overhead. A sudden breeze, brushing my arms warmed by the late afternoon sun, stirred the ivy leaves thickly covering the garden side of the house. I turned to see green layers ripple against old bricks. For a brief moment they seemed real, as did the breath of coolness on my skin. But what moved me was a vision of other leaves blown by other winds against another wall. I knew then, know now, that my present self lives for the sole purpose of watching, waiting, and listening, in a darkened hall, while fleeting scenes and fragments of music reach me from the past, which alone is real to me.

Buried deep in every heart, sometimes almost forgotten, rests a little, framed stage with glazed screen. Within this shadow box the treasures of childhood live. When I turn up the lamps to see through my own distant glass, it is always summertime on the farther side. Wisps of dust curl around the running feet of a younger self, since lost. A hot sun burns my skin, I hear the whisper of a thousand leaves, and a fragrance of crushed herbs and flowers reaches me from far away. The present fades, leaving me alone with the past once more.

An orchestra fills the galleried temple of my mind. A myriad Chinese wind harps hanging there crowd it with pendant prisms.

The events of the day, like moving currents of air, sway the peripheral chimes. When two strike against each other, the overtones they make, immediate and clear, go unheeded. My ear waits for harmonics evoked in the depths of the crystal forest. The inner music is memory.

If today I could see the grass of China bending to a storm, the harp's first notes would ring loud enough to hush the echoed harmony. Instead I hear that inner music each day long—for the whip of a bitter wind cutting my wrists like a razor blade turns to Peking's biting gales whistling all winter out of the Gobi Desert. The smell of water filling the tub, or the flavor of cucumber when I taste it as though for the first time takes me home to Hwaiyuen. Sunlight and shadow moving beneath a tree or the ruffling of vine leaves on a wall, small waves lapping against pebbles on a beach, a goldfish swimming in a bowl, even the color blue, are like hearing, suddenly and unexpectedly, the voice of a loved one thought dead. The music never stops.

Friends tell me that going back to scenes once cherished is enough to mute the chimes. For them it may be the case, since they all began life here in America and the path to an earlier home is open to each of them. But I was born on a distant shore. Though I left it many years ago I wait impatiently for the day when I can return. Until then my memory will play for me, over and over again, the plainsongs of my youth.

I think of those early years with great tenderness. I cannot say whether it was the quality of childhood itself, or the country in which I lived that gave those times their special flavor. Do those faraway days seem more real to me than the present because the world in which I grew up had not yet been scarred by modern man and his "progress"? Until I came to America I saw no billboards, no neon signs, raw excavations or ugly buildings, no heaps of rusting rubble. Instead, the cared-for face of China swept with ancient grace from plain to mountain. Across the breadth of land, proud trees sheltered temples and thatched roofs of scattered farmhouses, or arched across walls along town streets to shade the passerby. A sense of serenity governed the pace at which we lived and bathed the landscape around us in muted browns, grays and blues, the cool colors of the Orient. These hues were old and faded, their subtle nuances played upon by clear light.

An antique culture's hand gently shaped my spirit while I grew up and fell in love with the land I knew. Ever since I came to this new world, I have longed to walk again through fragrant gardens I remember, to be present when summer dawns wake the sleeping shores of Peitaiho, to see my homeland, its rivers, mountains, fields, its sand and soil. They cannot change. Roads may disappear, and temples be razed, but surely no man could or would erase the scenes to which, one day, I must return!

Now I consider the charm of youth itself. Was it that alone which seasoned my recollections? Was it the sense of weightlessness, of being unfettered, that gave my days their effortless flow? When a child, I bore no burdens. The virgin hours unfurled before me, blank scrolls, each to be covered with crisp line drawings before I rolled them up again at evening to store them with other memories.

During the years that have elapsed since then, the weight of time and cares and waiting to return have slowed my step. There is no tedium like waiting. At last the heart, like a weary palimpsest, resists all efforts made to draw one single further line upon its surface.

So when I look at Breughel's painting of the harvest I see beyond its surface a different medieval world. Asian fields of corn and kaoliang burn amber in the sun, and Chinese peasants thresh grain or lie down to rest in spots of umber shade.

The winter scene becomes a sheet of ice through which I see Hwaiyuen's snow-covered hills, black-veined by barren branches of wild pomegranate trees.

The chasm between the ancient and the modern world is awesome to cross. Perhaps my spirit quailed and refused to travel with my body. I think it more likely, however, that it came along with me, but on seeing the new world, fled back to the old, leaving me behind to get along without it, or follow it home.

So my spirit waits for me. Across many, many miles of sea and land I feel its great, magnetic pull. My longing to rejoin it, and all things Chinese, has been growing stronger year by year. And that is why, once again, I have taken to making Chinese rugs as I did a decade ago when nostalgia's first pangs hit me so very hard.

Contents

Introduction   1

How to Make Your Own Graph   6

Some Suggestions for Changes   8

Tips on Working   9

Finishing a Rug   10

Phoenix Rug   16

Cash or Money Rug   22

Pony Rug   30

Fabulous Border Rug   36

Foo Lion Rug   46

Classic Peony Rug   54

Garniture Rug   62

Fish Medallion Rug   80

Flying Cranes Rug   88

Elephant Panel   96

Bibliography   111

Wool Requirements

Phoenix Rug   page 16

Background quantity: Approximately 2 lbs.

Money Rug   page 22

Background quantity: Approximately 1½ lbs.
Other quantities: Approximately ¾ lb. white
Approximately ¾ lb. light
Approximately ½ lb. medium
Approximately ½ lb. medium dark

Pony Rug   page 30

Background quantity: Approximately 1¾ lbs.

Fabulous Border Rug   page 36

Quantities: Approximately ½ lb. white
Approximately 1 lb. medium
Approximately 1½ lbs. dark

Foo Lion Rug page 46

Background quantity: Approximately 1¾ lbs. Tête de Nègre
Approximately 1 lb. white
Approximately ½ lb. medium light
Approximately ½ lb. medium
Approximately 1 ounce medium accent color

Classic Peony Rug page 54

Background quantities: Approximately 2 lbs. light
Approximately 2 lbs. medium

Garniture Rug page 62

Background quantity: Approximately 4 lbs.

Fish Medallion Rug page 80

Background quantity: Approximately 5 lbs.
Other quantities: Approximately 1½ lbs. white
Approximately 1 lb. dark

Flying Cranes Rug page 88

Background quantity: Approximately 1¾ lbs.
Other quantities: Approximately 1 lb. white
Approximately ¾ lb. light
Approximately 1 lb. medium dark

Elephant Rug or Panel page 96

Background quantity: Approximately 2½ lbs.
Elephant quantity: Approximately ¾ lb.

Introduction

Rugs make a much more powerful statement than do pillows, perhaps because they are larger. To me a rug is like a novel, a pillow a short story. Therefore to all you ardent needleworkers who have "read enough short stories" for the time being, and now want to try something bigger, I suggest a "novel"—make a rug. So I extend to you the invitation to look through the pages of this book. Here you will find many designs for Chinese rugs. If the exact size and shape of rug you need are missing from my collection, the designs are planned so that you can rearrange details and borders to suit your taste. Color schemes, too, can be changed. A later chapter deals with this subject.

It takes no special courage to make a rug, only time— perhaps as long as it takes to make five or six pillows. If you are familiar with my first two books, *Needlepoint by Design*, and *More Needlepoint by Design*, you already know how to work from a graph. You also know that if you do not make any mistakes in counting, the end results are going to measure up to your expectations.

For those of you who have never worked from a graph, and need help, let me explain the process here.

Every graph in this book represents a design with all finished stitches in their proper places. If you will look closely at a piece of needlepoint, you will observe a gridwork of fine, slightly wavy vertical and horizontal lines running up, down, and across its surface. This grid outlines the stitches. Each stitch looks like a fat grain of rice perched, slightly tilted, in the grid. A graph is simply a mechanical version of a piece of finished work. Instead of the slightly wavy gridlines appearing on a piece of finished needlework, the gridlines on a graph have been "ironed out" so that the stitches they outline are small squares rather than ovals. Many people are confused by a graph, thinking the gridlines represent the threads of their canvas. They wonder, when looking at the graph, why they cannot understand where the needle should come up and go down, either in the graph or on their canvases. I suggest to these people that they think of it this way: *The needle will come up at the lower left-hand corner of the little graph square —or stitch—and go down at the upper right-hand corner of the same little graph square—or stitch.* Make a stitch on your canvas. Think of it as corresponding to a little square on the graph. Then you will see that the holes in your canvas are *really* represented by the *corners* of the graph squares. When you work needlepoint from a graph, you are, in a sense, working needlepoint by the numbers. You are following a design of small squares on a graph and reproducing them as stitches on your canvas.

After reading and understanding the above paragraph, you will perceive that before you start stitching, you could make counting from a graph much easier if you marked your canvas with lines corresponding to the heavy lines on the graph. These occur every tenth line. On your canvas you must draw these lines *between the threads*. When you have completed marking your canvas, each square block outlined on the canvas will contain room for 100 stitches, just as each square block on the graph contains 100 small squares.

The graph thread-count is given at the beginning of the second paragraph of each set of instructions for a rug. When the thread-count is uneven—that is, when the numbers are odd numbers—mark the centers of your canvas *along* the horizontal and vertical center threads of your canvas. When the thread-count is even—that is, when the numbers are even numbers—mark the centers of your canvas *between* two threads at the horizontal and vertical centers of your canvas.

To help keep you from getting lost when reading from graph to canvas, you can key them even more completely. Write num-

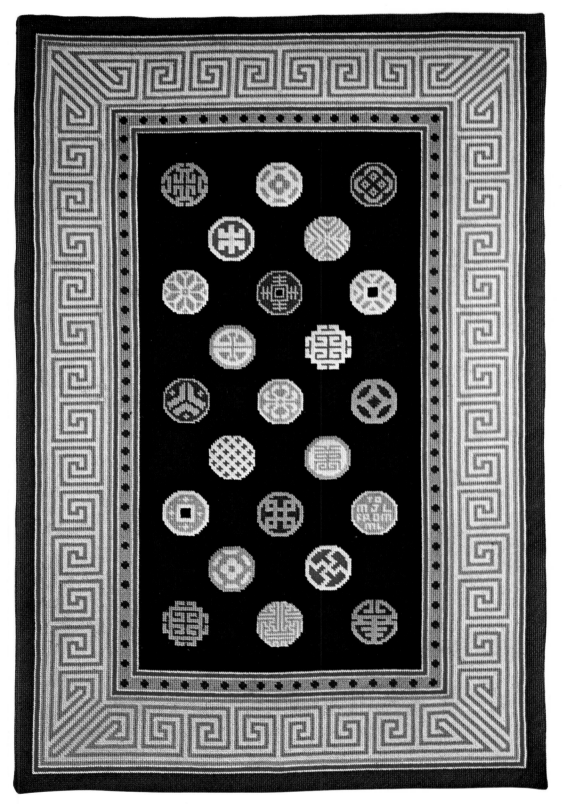

Cash or Money Rug   see pages 22-29

Phoenix Rug   see pages 16-21

Detail of Phoenix

Pony Rug   see pages 30-35

Fabulous Border Rug   see pages 36-45

Foo Lion Rug   see pages 46-53

Detail of Foo Lion

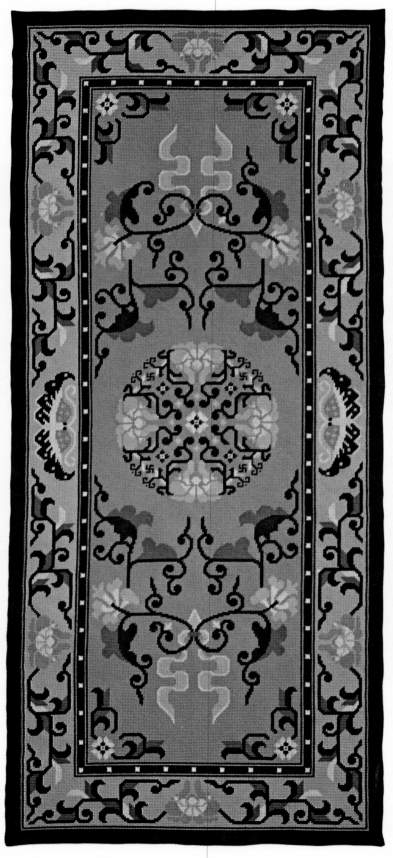

Classic Peony Rug   see pages 54-61

Garniture Rug   see pages 62-79

Garniture Rug (enlargement)

Fish Medallion Rug   see pages 80-87

Detail of Fish Medallion

Elephant Panel   see pages 96–109

Detail of Elephant

Flying Cranes Rug   see pages 88-95

bers along both sides of your canvas and your graph so that the numbers on the canvas correspond to the numbers on the graph. Write letters across both the top and the bottom of both canvas and graph so that the letters on the canvas correspond to the letters on the graph.

The pen to use for marking needlepoint canvas should be waterproof. I have found Sharpies to be a good brand. These felt-tipped pens are available in primary colors as well as in brown and black. I choose to use brown rather than black, which I find too dark. A medium gray or beige would be better for marking canvas, but as yet I have not found a sharp, indelible, felt-tipped pen in either of these two colors.

Bind your canvas with masking tape, or make a narrow folded hem on each side of your canvas, and sew it flat, either by machine or by hand. Otherwise the wool thread you use for work will constantly snag on the rough edge of your canvas. The canvas will also unravel if you do not bind it.

Use a needle with an eye big enough for easy threading. The size will vary according to the mesh of the canvas on which you plan to work. I find 16 to be a comfortable needle size for both #8 and #10 canvas, but I suggest that you experiment and find the needle size that suits your needs best.

Some of you may find the graphs in the book a little too small for easy reading. If this is the case, a photostat of any graph can be enlarged to provide you with a larger grid, and easier reading.

You may want to color the graphs you choose to use. I would suggest a set of coloring pencils for this purpose.

When you are ready to make the first stitch on your canvas, I strongly recommend that you mark, on the graph, the block of stitches containing your starting point. Then, most carefully, locate the corresponding block of stitches on your canvas. *Mark it immediately*. Otherwise you may, while threading your needle, lose it and have to find it all over again. If, in spite of checking and double-checking the location of the starting point, you find that you are off by a whole block, do not despair. There is a remedy. (And it is not ripping!) You can simply redraw the center lines and the outlines of your rug to allow for your error. This is one good reason for leaving several inches of blank canvas around your planned work area.

Needlepoint canvas comes in several widths. Those of interest to the rug maker are 36″ wide, 40″ wide, and 60″ wide. To my knowledge, no one makes a canvas wider than 60″. If you want to make a rug much wider than 54″, after allowing 3″ extra on either side—which brings the total width to 60″—you will need to piece it. *None of the designs in this book require piecing.* Each one has been designed to be worked on an existing canvas width.

If you plan to graph or make your own rug design, or to rescale one of the designs in this book, using a different canvas mesh than that used in the sample rug, the following figures will help you:

36″ canvas

#10 mono canvas gives you	300 usable threads
#9 Penelope canvas gives you	270 " "
#8 Penelope canvas gives you	240 " "
#7 Penelope canvas gives you	210 " "

60″ canvas

#10 mono canvas gives you	510 " "
#9 Penelope canvas gives you	490 " "
#8 Penelope canvas gives you	465 " "
#5 Quick-point Penelope gives you	270 " "

Both these sets of figures allow for 3″ of extra canvas at each side of the given count.

The following list of usable threads per canvas width and mesh will be helpful if you want to rescale any rug. Keep in mind, always, the graph thread-count given in paragraph two of each set of instructions:

510 Usable threads	=	10 mono canvas		60″ width
490 " "	=	9 Penelope canvas		60″ "
465 " "	=	8 Penelope canvas		60″ "
300 " "	=	10 mono canvas		36″ "
270 " "	=	9 Penelope canvas		36″ "
270 " "	=	5 " Quick-point		60″ "
240 " "	=	8 Penelope canvas		36″ "
210 " "	=	7 Penelope canvas		36″ "

The width and mesh of the canvas you choose for your rug give you the only limitation you need consider when graphing a rug. You can make a rug as long as you like simply by buying the lengthwise yardage you need, plus extra length for blocking and hemming. But you *must* take into account the number of usable threads *across* the canvas, for this number cannot be changed, unless you choose a canvas with more threads to the inch—that is, a canvas with a finer weave.

Amount of wool needed for each rug: ¼ lb or 1 skein will cover approximately 1 square foot of canvas. The only color you need worry about when it comes to dye lots is the background color. If you do not have enough of any of the other colors to finish the rug, simply buy more. Different dye lots will *not* be discernible in patterned areas, whereas they could be apparent when worked in a plain field. Even in large areas, however, a remedy is available if you find your supply of background color is not going to be enough for finishing the background. Save some of it, order more, and when the new batch of wool comes, take one strand of the new and use it with the old, (removing one strand of the old). Work with this combination of new and old for a few rows. Then use two strands of new in place of two strands of old. Work for a few rows. Finally use all new wool. This will ease the transition from one dye lot to another and soften what might otherwise be an abrupt and discernible, even though slight, change in color or tonal value.

How to Make Your Own Graph

Sheets of graph paper measuring 18″ x 21″ are available in many art stores. Buy the kind with 10 lines to the running inch, or 100 small squares to the square inch. (If you plan to work on #10 mono canvas, your graph will then be about equal in size to the finished rug. If you plan to work on #8 Penelope canvas, the graph will, of course, be smaller than the finished rug.) Trim the sheets of graph paper before pasting them together to approximate the size of the rug you wish to make. NOTE: I then turn over the resulting large sheet of joined graph paper and reinforce the seams with Scotch Magic Tape. Masking tape will eventually stain the graph paper with a yellow oil, so it should not be used as a reinforcement on paper.

If you plan to adapt designs presented in this book, decide first which part of the border contains the motif with a fixed number of stitches. The swastika, for example, uses a fixed number of stitches. When it is repeated, that fixed number is added for every repeat. Therefore, when making a design either wider, narrower, longer, or shorter, bear in mind the fixed number needed for the motif in the repeat border you have chosen to use.

You should graph this part of the rug border first. Usually you need graph only a quarter of a border, for once you know where the centers of your design will be, you can outline the whole work area, then the field. Once the latter is established you can arrange motifs and details on it in any way you desire.

6

When planning your rug you may wish to use a different approach. Instead of following the method I have just described— from graph to canvas—you may want to reverse the process and plan from canvas to graph. If that be the case, buy your canvas first. Outline on it an area the size of the rug you wish to make. Count the number of horizontal and vertical threads within this outline. *Don't forget to leave three inches of blank canvas around your planned work area.* After establishing the horizontal and vertical thread-count, outline this same thread-count on your graph paper. Proceed to graph your border pattern. (Again, you usually need to graph only a quarter of your border.) Then re-outline the entire work area on your graph. This will be figured on the basis of the thread-count you have established in the graphed quarter of the border. Outline the field. Now, again, you have freedom in the field. (When you go back to your canvas, turn it over, and on its blank side, outline your corrected work area, based on the thread-count you have arrived at in your finished graph.)

I sketch directly on the graph paper. When I am satisfied with my design, I then begin "step-drawing"—that is, outlining the motifs and separating the color areas, always using a zigzag line that follows the graph lines. This method produces drawings like those in this book.

Even if you cannot draw well you can, with help, graph any design or motif you like. Simply have it photostated and enlarged to the size you need for your graph. Then make a tracing of it on tracing paper. To transfer this tracing to your graph paper, blacken the back side of your tracing by rubbing the paper with a very soft lead pencil point. Place the tracing over your graph paper and redraw your design with a sharp pencil. When you lift your tracing paper, you will see that you have transferred to your graph paper a ghostly copy of your original drawing.

Some Suggestions for Changes
That Can Easily Be Made
in the Existing Rug Designs

Whenever a small repeat pattern—like that in the Pony rug border —has been used, another small repeat pattern can be substituted for it. The tonal values in these small repeat patterns can also be changed—that is, you can use light where I have used dark, and dark where I have used light. This completely changes the character and tonal value of the patterns.

The central motif in a rug may be eliminated, or another used in its place. (These same central motifs can be used as designs for circular pillows.) A rug's plain field can be changed by using an all-over pattern worked in close tones. Square rugs can be lengthened, long rugs made square. And the coins in the Money rug, when worked on #7 canvas, could make handsome coasters.

The Elephant rug, which is shown as a vertical panel, can be made into a horizontal rug by working the wave border on both sides of the elephant rather than below it. This same wave border can also be substituted for the tassel design appearing at the top of the Elephant rug. In fact, you could use the elephant as a central motif on a rug and surround it with a square or rectangular border.

Your ingenuity will surely suggest to you many other possibilities that I have never even imagined. So, if you like, be bold and make changes, for I am giving you, here in this book, a modular system. Like a set of building blocks, it is meant to be used with pleasure to create unique and personal designs. I do hope you enjoy working with it.

8

Tips on Working

When working on a rug use only those stitches that will least distort your canvas. I recommend the basket weave and the brick stitch. *Never use the continental stitch* except for single rows of stitching where no other stitch can be used. The continental stitch distorts canvas so much that it is *totally* inappropriate for a piece of needlework that will be expected to remain rectangular without the help of a frame or some other form of rigid support.

Use as many strands of wool as you need to cover the canvas with an easy stitch—that is, a stitch made without a tug to tighten it. If you work with a hard pull at the end of each stitch, no amount of blocking can permanently correct the final result—a crooked canvas. Such a piece of work will stay rectangular *only* if mounted on a rigid frame which will counteract the tension you have created with your repeated tugging. A rug is destined to lie freely on the floor. Be kind to it when you work on it. Work with an easy, flowing rhythm and a stitch that does little to distort a rectangle. *Do not work with a hard tug at the end of each stitch.* If you follow these suggestions, your rug will need little blocking.

Do not allow your thread to twist and loop while you work. To keep it straight, roll the needle a bit between stitches. You will soon discover how to do this. An untwisted thread makes for smoother stitches.

When you finish a thread, turn to the back of your work and run the needle and thread under almost a full needle's length of stitches before clipping off the thread's tail. Do the same when anchoring a new thread.

Finishing a Rug

During the entire period that I am working on a rug I press it almost daily, using a damp cloth and a hot iron. While doing this, I pull the needlework to straighten it as much as possible. As a result, when the stitching on the rug has been completed, the finished piece is almost rectangular. But no matter how rectangular it appears, a rug should be blocked before being hemmed, bound, and lined.

Many needlepoint shops will perform these finishing services for you. However, if you want to finish a rug yourself, the following directions may be of help.

Blocking a Rug

Before blocking a rug, first clip the selvages on the canvas unless you have already removed them. The selvage is the tightly woven lengthwise edge of the canvas. Unless removed or clipped, it will pucker these edges of the canvas and prevent your rug from lying flat. Clip through the selvage, every inch or so, making short nips only half an inch deep. This will ease the tension along the lengthwise edges of the canvas.

Lay the rug face up on a board or a large wooden stretcher, made 4″ longer and 4″ wider than your rug. I have made such stretchers with four 2″ x 4″ wooden strips, which I have strengthened at the corners by means of screwing on flat, L-shaped angle irons, available at most hardware stores.

10

Do not wet the rug before blocking it. This would only cause it to tighten up and go askew, making the blocking process very difficult, if not impossible. Instead, tack the dry canvas to the four corners of the frame. The 3″ border of raw canvas that you left around your work will now perform part of its function. You will drive *long carpet tacks* into the canvas instead of into the needlework. (If you have a staple gun, you can use staples instead of carpet tacks.)

After lightly anchoring the four corners of your canvas, start tacking the four edges, beginning at the center of each side. Do not tack a whole side at once. Instead, with a short row of tacks, anchor the centers of the four sides, then, circling around the rug, and always pulling from the center out, keep tacking. Pull evenly so as to eliminate all ripples. Tack at 1″ intervals until you reach the corners. If you run into stubborn areas of stitches that refuse to lie flat, use a steam iron and shoot steam at these spots. This will make pulling easier. When you have finished tacking, the rug should be rectangular and as taut as a drum.

At this point, dampen the rug thoroughly. Then leave it on the stretcher for at least 24 hours, or until it is totally free of moisture—bone dry.

Remove the rug from the stretcher. If it goes slightly askew, do not be alarmed. Many rugs need more than one blocking. If yours is one of these, be patient and repeat the process described above. (Two blockings should be enough.)

Once a rug remains rectangular upon removal from its rigid supports, it is ready for hemming, binding, and lining.

Hemming a Rug

Trim off 1″ of canvas all the way around the rug, leaving 2″ for hemming. At each corner, cut off a triangle of canvas. Allow about ½″ of canvas between the hypotenuse of each triangle—the diagonal cutting line—and each corner of your finished needlework. Lay the rug face down on a flat surface. Fold in the four diagonal edges at the four corners, bringing the fold lines up to the corners of the needlework. Press. Then fold in the four side flaps. Press. Where the flaps meet diagonally at the corners you

12

have what is known as a mitered corner. Sew these diagonal corner seams, using a strong thread. Then use a backstitch to sew the four sides of canvas hem to the under side of your rug.

Turn the rug over. There should be no raw canvas showing. The edges should be straight and flat, and the corners neat and true.

Binding a Rug

Take a skein of wool. *Cut it once.* Thread your needle, pull the thread halfway through so that the thread hangs in two equally long tails from the needle's eye. Turn the point of the needle back on the tails and pierce both of them as close to the needle as possible. Draw the needle through the pierced threads. Smooth the joining of the threads. You now have a double thread that will not slip in the needle's eye. This method of threading a needle will facilitate binding because a needle with one thread through its eye will slide through the canvas much more easily than one with two threads through its eye.

Begin binding at a corner of the rug. Run the needle in and out a few times on the canvas hem under the rug. Backstitch if you want to anchor the thread more firmly. Then begin whipping the edge of the rug. Hold the rug with its edge up and the under side of your needlework toward you. Make your stitches from the right side of the rug toward the under side. Your binding will whip and wrap the outermost row of needlepoint and the first row of raw canvas underneath. Work over each stitch on the top edge and through each matching hole underneath, making a tight spiral. The double whipping thread will produce a neat, rolled edge. Keep the whipping threads from twisting. When casting off at the ends of the whipping threads, or when anchoring new ones, weave the ends into the raw canvas hem. Again, backstitch if you wish to anchor the threads more firmly. Continue whipping, casting off, and beginning new threads in the described manner until you have whipped a rolled edge around the entire rug.

NOTE: When binding a rug, as when working the stitches on a rug, *do not work with a tight stitch* or you will produce a whipping that ripples and undulates rather than one that lies flat.

Lining a Rug

Buy a piece of heavy cotton, like sailcloth, or a piece of tightly woven linen, preferably of a neutral beige color. Cut the fabric to a size about 4″ longer and 4″ wider than your finished rug. Fold in 2″ along two adjoining sides of the lining. Miter the resulting corner. Lay the rug face down on a flat surface. Place the lining on the back of the rug so that the two folded edges of the lining meet the inner edges of the whipping along two sides of the rug. Pin the lining to the whipping along these two sides. Then turn under the remaining two sides of the lining so they meet the other two inner edges of whipping on the other two sides of the rug. Miter the three remaining corners of the lining. Pin the lining to the whipping, then catch-stitch the lining to the whipping, all the way around the rug.

While the rug is still lying face down, tack the lining to the rug by means of a row of basting stitches running all the way around the sides of the rectangle, but 2″ from the edges. Then tack the center of the lining to the center of the rug, using a large horizontal and vertical cross-stitch and a large diagonal cross-stitch. These tacking stitches will keep the lining from creeping and showing around the edges of the rug, once it lies face up upon the floor.

NOTE: It is wise to place a piece of rubber matting under your needlepoint rug to keep it from slipping on the floor. The matting should be about 4″ narrower and 4″ shorter than the rug. To keep the rug and the matting properly aligned, tack the ends of four strips of tape diagonally across the underside corners of your rug. Slip the corners of the matting into these traps. Or make four triangular pockets at the four underside corners of your rug. Sew them in about an inch from the edges. Slip the corners of the matting into these pockets.

The retail mail-order source I recommend for all canvases and wools listed in this book is: Boutique Margot, 26 West 54th Street, New York, New York 10019.

All wool used in the sample rugs is Paternayan's three-ply Persian yarn.

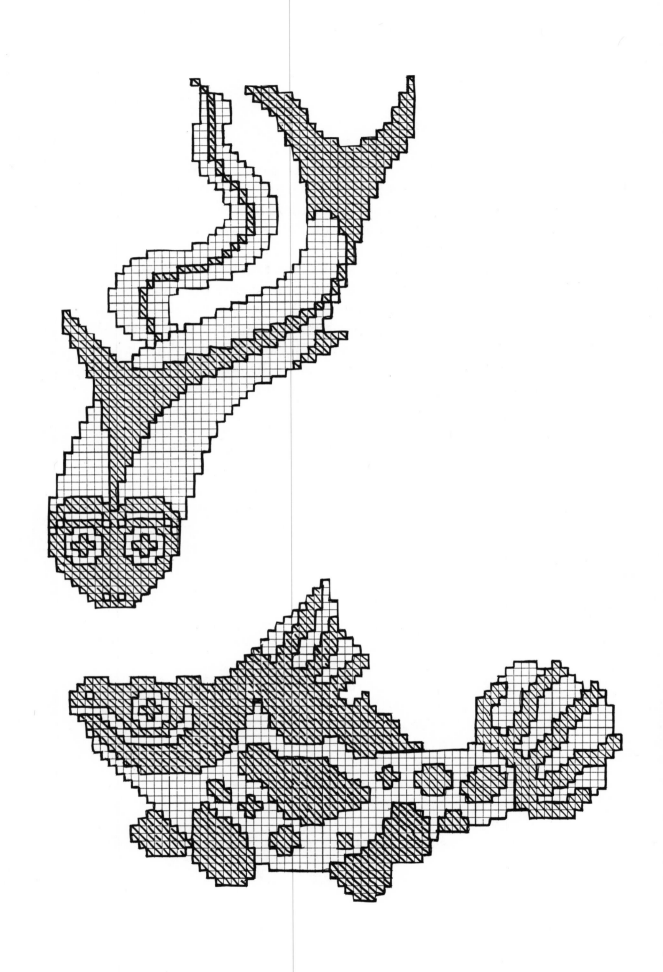

The Rug Designs

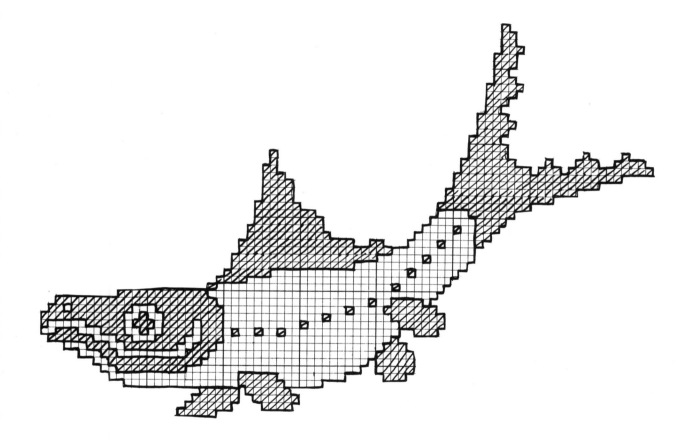

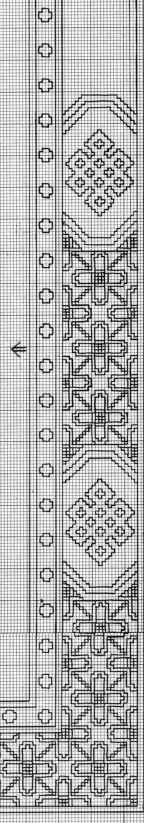

ARROW REPRESENTS CENTER THREAD

TOP

BOTTOM

Phoenix Rug

40″ x 40″

Worked on #8 Penelope canvas
Wool needed, see page xii

This design was adapted from a roundel made for a Ming Dynasty empress. The original is in the possession of the Metropolitan Museum of Art. The border was adapted from an antique Mongolian rug border.

The graph thread-count is 311 x 311. Bind off a piece of #8 Penelope canvas measuring 46″ x 46″. Mark center lines and outline work area. Mark graph lines for the Phoenix roundel. You should not find them necessary for working the border.

The sample rug was made with Persian wool, using the full thread, all three strands. If you want a rug with a tight weave, add one extra strand of wool to the three-strand thread. You will then be working with four strands.

Eleven colors and tones were used in the Phoenix rug. The key follows:

1. 012 White
2. 396 Palest blue
3. 395 Light blue
4. 386 Medium light blue
5. 430 Light salmon
6. 420 Salmon
7. 563 Light celadon green
8. 573 Dark celadon green
9. 134 Brown—background color
10. 114 Dark brown
11. 304 Black navy

18

1. Work the Phoenix roundel, using sample rug as a key to color and tonal value.
2. Work pearl border.
3. Work background of field, 134 brown.
4. Work white outline at outer edge of patterned border.
5. Work outlines of lozenges containing eternal knots.
6. Work eternal knots, then fill in with background color, 134 brown.
7. Work patterned border, using sample rug as a key to color and tonal value.
8. Work background of patterned border, 134 brown.
9. Work final outer border.

Sample rug worked by Candy McCandliss.

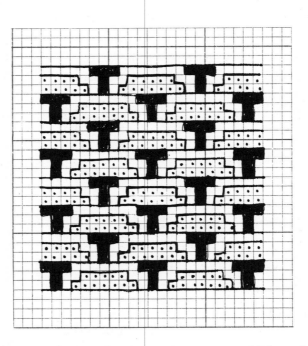

Detail of body of Phoenix. See color plates of Phoenix, the second and third color plates.

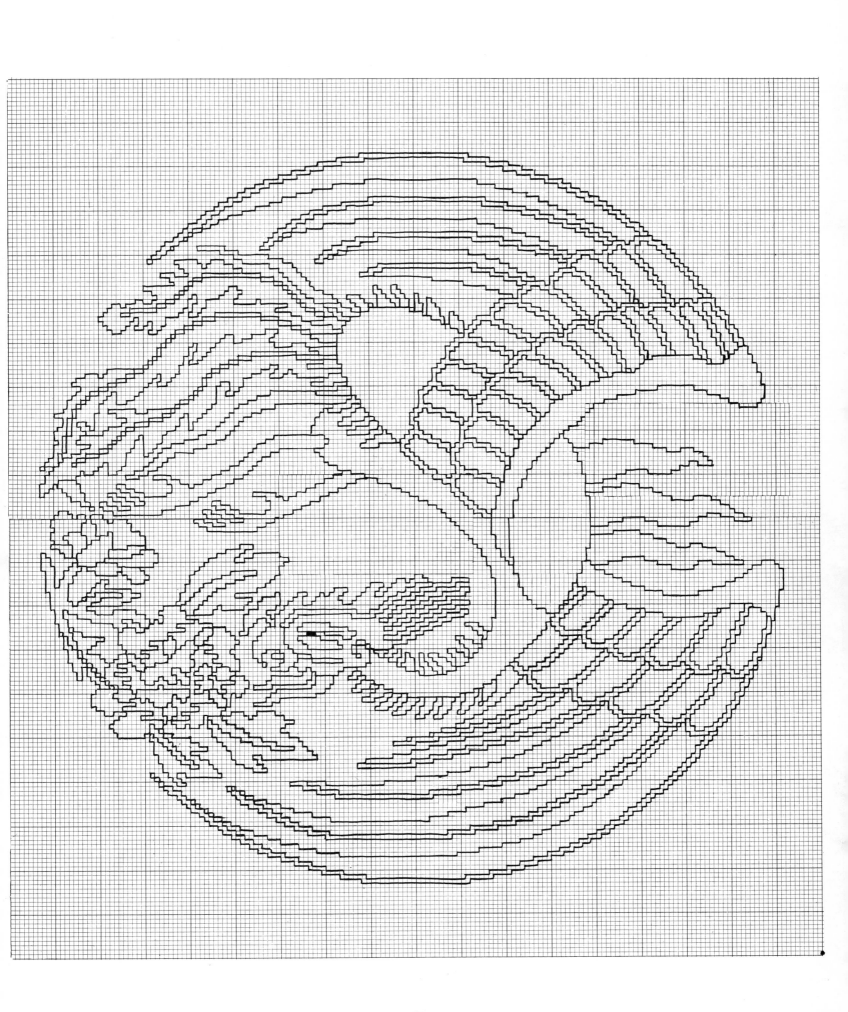

Cash or Money Rug

33″ x 50″

Worked on #8 Penelope canvas
Wool needed, see page xii

This design was adapted from an antique Mongol saddle rug.

The graph thread-count is 264 x 402. Bind off a piece of #8 Penelope canvas measuring 39″ x 56″. Mark center lines and outline work area. Mark graph lines for the field. You should not need them for the rest of the rug.

Five tones are used in the Cash or Money rug. They are:

1. White
2. Light
3. Medium
4. Medium dark
5. Dark

The sample rug was made with Persian wool, using the full thread, all three strands. If you want a rug with a tight weave, add one extra strand of wool to the three-strand thread. You will then be working with four strands.

The key to the colors used in the sample rug follows:

1. 010 Off-white
2. 479 Chamois gold
3. 330 Blue
4. 583 Olive brown
5. 304 Black navy

1. Using tones #1, #2, #3, and #4, work the coins as shown in the sample rug.
2. Using tones #1, #2, #3, and #4, work pearl border.

3. Using tone #5, work background of field.
4. Using tones #1 and #3, work bands at outer edge of key-fret border.
5. Using tone #1, work key fret.
6. Using tone #2, fill in background of key-fret border.
7. Using tone #4, work final outer border.

The sample rug was worked by Maggie Lane and Louise de Paoli.

NOTE: The coins, when worked individually on #7 canvas, will make nice coasters.

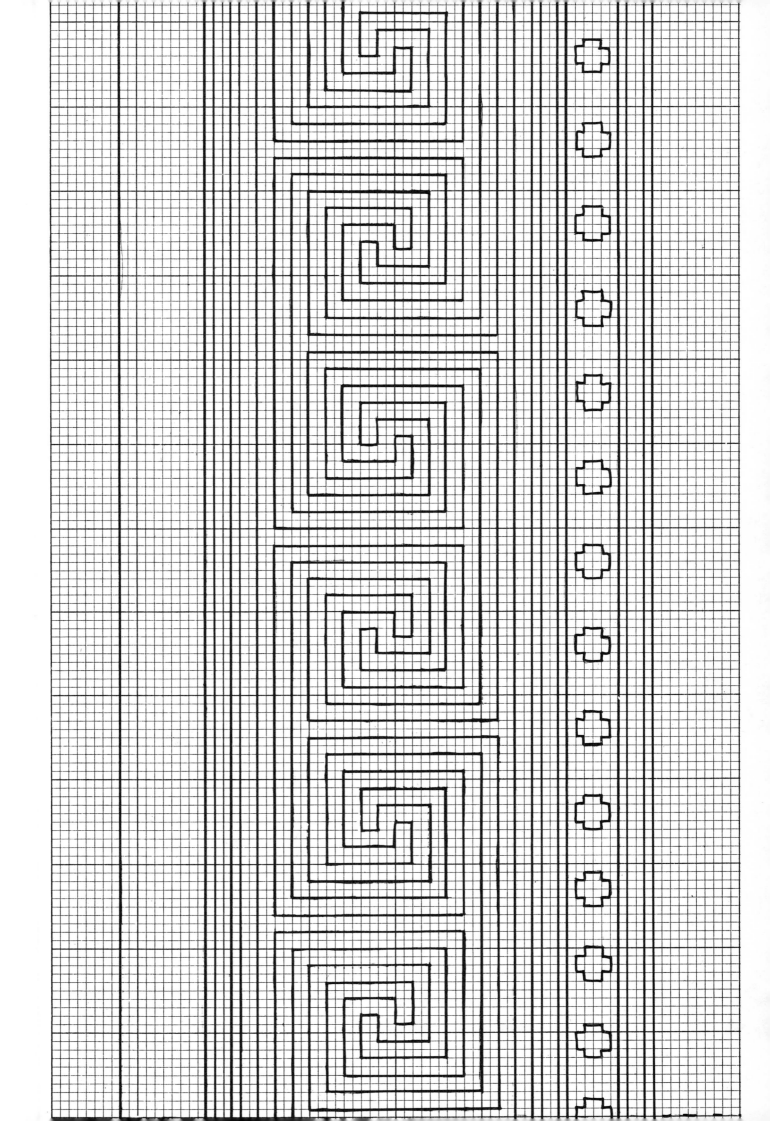

Pony Rug

23″ x 49″

Worked on #8 Penelope canvas
Wool needed, see page xii

This design was adapted from a 19th-century Suiyuan rug, plate 83 in *A View of Chinese Rugs* by H. A. Lorentz, Routledge and Kegan Paul, Ltd., publishers.

The graph thread-count is 181 x 391. Bind off a piece of #8 Penelope canvas measuring 29″ x 56″. Mark center lines and outline work area. The graph presents only one lengthwise half of the rug, but you will use it for both lengthwise halves. Therefore, starting at one end, mark graph lines on only one lengthwise half of the canvas, ending below the two clouds in the center of the rug. Then turn the canvas and repeat the process. Mark graph lines for the clouds only when you are ready to work them. This will eliminate confusion.

Five tones are used in the Pony rug. They are:

1. White
2. Light
3. Medium light
4. Medium
5. Dark

The sample rug was made with Persian wool, using the full thread, all three strands. If you want a rug with a tight weave, add one extra strand of wool to the three-strand thread. You will then be working with four strands.

31

The key to the colors used in the sample rug follows:

1. 017 Off-white
2. 396 Light blue
3. 395 Medium light blue
4. 386 Medium blue
5. 365 Dark blue

1. Using tone #5, outline the field. Using tone #2, work the row immediately outside the row just worked. Using tone #4, work the third, or outer row.
2. Work the waves at the bottom of the picture. Use tone #1 for the outline bands at the top of each wave. Use tone #5 for the second band. Use tone #4 for the third band, and tone #2 for the fourth band. Finish each wave using tones #4 and #2 for alternate bands.
3. Using tone #2, outline the row of stones appearing above the waves. Then work the little squares in each stone. Then fill in the stones, using tones #5, #3 and #4.
4. Using tones #1, #2 and #4, work the flowers growing out of the stones, and those standing free in the field above the stones.
5. Using tone #4 for the trunk, and tone #2 for the flowers, work the small tree at the left.
6. Using tone #2 for the body and tone #1 for the wings, work the butterfly above the small tree.
7. Work the pony.

   Using tone #1, outline the pony's eye, work the bridle, the pommels of the saddle, and the field of the saddle rug. Using tone #2, work the outline between the pony's body and the hind leg. Also, work the tail, hoofs, mane, and the saddle between the pommels.

   Using tone #3, work the tassel below the chest, outline the saddle rug, and work the serrated crupper between saddle rug and the pony's tail.

   Using tone #5, work the stirrup, the pony's nostril, and the pupil of his eye.

   Using tone #4, work the body of the pony.

8. Using tone #4 for the trunk, and tone #2 for the bunches of feathered leaves, work the large tree at the right of the field.

9. Using tone #1, outline the two clouds, then fill in with tone #4.

10. Using tone #5, fill in the field.

11. Using tone #1, work dots around field.

12. Using tone #4, work key-fret band.

13. Using tone #5, work background of dot and key-fret band.

14. Using tone #5, work outer border.

15. Using tones #2, #4 and #5, fill in patterned border.

16. Using tone #5, work the dark pattern in horizontal or vertical rows. Then, using tone #2, work the small stars. Finally, using tone #4, fill in the rest of the pattern.

Sample rug worked by Maggie Lane and Louise de Paoli.

Fabulous Border Rug

28″ x 56″

Worked on #8 Penelope canvas
Wool needed, see page xii

This design was adapted from an antique Chinese rug.

The graph thread-count is 229 x 451. Bind off a piece of #8 Penelope canvas measuring 34″ x 62″. Mark center lines and outline work area. Mark graph lines for the entire rug.

Four tones are used in the Fabulous Border rug. They are:

1. White
2. Light
3. Medium
4. Dark

The sample rug was made with Persian wool, using the full thread, all three strands. If you want a rug with a tight weave, add one extra strand of wool to the three-strand thread. You will then be working with four strands.

The key to the colors used in the sample rug follows:

1. 010 Off-white
2. 563 Light celadon green
3. 583 Medium celadon green
4. 573 Dark celadon green

1. Using tone #1, work two-row band outlining field.
2. Using tones #1, #3, and #4, work center motif and four corner motifs.
3. Using tone #4, work diaper pattern of interlocking swastikas in field.

4. Using tone #3, work background of field.
5. Using tones #1, and #4, work key fret band outlining field. Using tone #3, work outline around key-fret band.
6. Using tones #1 and #3, work light band at outer edge of Fabulous Border.
7. Using tones #1, #2, and #3, work objects in border.

NOTE: Use tone #2 only in the dotted areas of the five objects marked with dotted shading.

8. Using tone #4, work background of Fabulous Border, and outer border band.

Sample rug worked by Robert G. Taylor.

OUTER BORDER

KEY FRET

OUTER BORDER

Foo Lion Rug

32″ x 50″

Worked on #10 mono canvas
Wool needed, see page xiii

This design was adapted from a Chinese rug belonging to Mr. and Mrs. Wagner, friends of my sister in St. Louis. The original rug had a dragon motif in the center. I chose to adapt and substitute for it a pair of Foo Lions found on a Ningshia chair rug, page 396 in *A Connoisseur's Guide to Oriental Rugs,* by E. Gans-Ruedin, Charles E. Tuttle, publishers.

The graph thread-count is 315 x 495. Bind off a piece of #10 mono canvas measuring 38″ x 56″. Mark center lines and outline work area. Mark graph lines for Foo Lions roundel. You should not need graph lines for the rest of the rug.

Four tones are used in the Foo Lions rug. They are:

1. White
2. Medium light
3. Medium
4. Dark

The sample rug was made with Persian wool, using the full thread, all three strands.

The key to the colors used in the sample rug follows:

1. 040 Old ivory
2. 440 Saffron yellow
3. 427 Pumpkin yellow
   (424 orange, for details only)
4. 105 Tête de nègre

1. Using tones #1, #3, and #4, work eyes of larger Foo Lion.
2. Using tones #1 and #4, work mouth of larger lion.

3. Using tone #1, work eyebrows and three lines on larger lion's nose.
4. Using tone #3, outline curls around larger lion's face, then fill in with #1 tone.
5. Using tone #3, fill in lion's face.
6. Using tone #3, work lines on larger lion's back and tail, then fill in with tone #1.
7. Using tone #3, work toenails on larger lion's paw, then work the paws with #1 tone.
8. Using tone #1, work lines in larger lion's legs and across the tummy. Work circular ball at top of the front leg. (It is a bell hanging around the neck.)
9. Using tone #4, work body and legs of larger lion.
10. Using tone #3, work toenails of smaller Foo Lion, then work under side of the ears and the center dots in the eyes.
11. Using tones #2 and #4, work smaller lion's eyes and mouth.
12. Using tone #2, work lines on smaller lion's face, then the lines on the back and tail.
13. Using tone #1, fill in smaller lion's back and tail, work paws and whiskers on the chin.
14. Using tone #2, fill in smaller lion's body. Don't forget the front right leg.
15. Using tone #2, work the curved outline and three decorative scrolls between smaller lion's head and larger lion's tail.
16. Using tone #1, work Eternal Knot in larger circular design, the ball in front of larger lion. Then work four spoke lines and the circle around them. Then outline the fluttering ribbon behind the ball.
17. Using tone #2, fill in the ball, except for the four grain-shaped areas. These will be worked in #4 tone (background color).
18. Using tone #3 (but the one reserved for details), work fluttering ribbon.
19. Using tone #1, outline cloud behind larger lion's head, then fill in with tone #3 (but the one reserved for details).

20. Using tone #4, fill in background in Foo Lions roundel.
21. Using tone #1, outline field area by working the three-row band. Work swastika border and outer three-row band.
22. Using tone #3, work the outlines of the hexagon pattern in the rug's field.
23. Using tone #2, outline smaller hexagons within the larger hexagons.
24. Using tone #2, work hearts of flowers in each hexagon.
25. Using tone #1, work flowers in each hexagon.
26. Using tone #4, fill in background of field and border.

This design is a horizontal one. If you turn the central motif and background pattern 90°, you can have a vertical design.

Sample rug worked by Maggie Lane and Louise de Paoli.

Classic Peony Rug

30″ x 70″

Worked on #8 Penelope canvas
Wool needed, see page xiii

This design was adapted from a 19th-century Chinese rug, plate 44 in *A View of Chinese Rugs*, by H. A. Lorentz, Routledge and Kegan Paul, Ltd., publishers.

The graph thread-count is 241 x 547. Bind off a piece of #8 Penelope canvas measuring 36″ x 76″. Mark center lines and outline work area. The graph presents only one lengthwise half of the rug, but you will use it for both lengthwise halves. Therefore, starting at one end, mark graph lines on only one lengthwise half of the canvas. Then continue marking graph lines for the center motif and the butterflies in the border. *Then stop.* Mark graph lines on second half of the rug only when you are ready to work that part of it. This will eliminate confusion.

Five tones are used in the Classic Peony rug. They are:

1. White
2. Light
3. Medum light
4. Medium
5. Dark

The sample rug was made with Persian wool, using the full thread, all three strands. If you want a rug with a tight weave, add one extra strand of wool to the three-strand thread. You will then be working with four strands.

The key to the colors used in the sample rug follows:

1. 010 Off-white
2. 593 Light olive
3. 590 Medium light olive
4. 553 Medium olive
5. 540 Dark olive

1. Using tones #1, #2, #4, and #5, work the center motif, the two corner motifs, and the large motif of flowers, leaves, and fluttering ribbons. Turn the canvas. Mark graph lines for second half of the field. Then work the two corner motifs and the large motif of flowers, leaves, and fluttering ribbons on the second half of the field.
2. Using tone #3, fill in background of field.
3. Using tones #1, #3, and #5, work pearl border around field.
4. Using tones #1, #3, #4, and #5, work leaves, flowers, and butterflies in border pattern.
5. Using tone #2, fill in background of border.
6. Using tones #2 and #5, work outer border bands.

Sample rug worked by Lois Cowles.

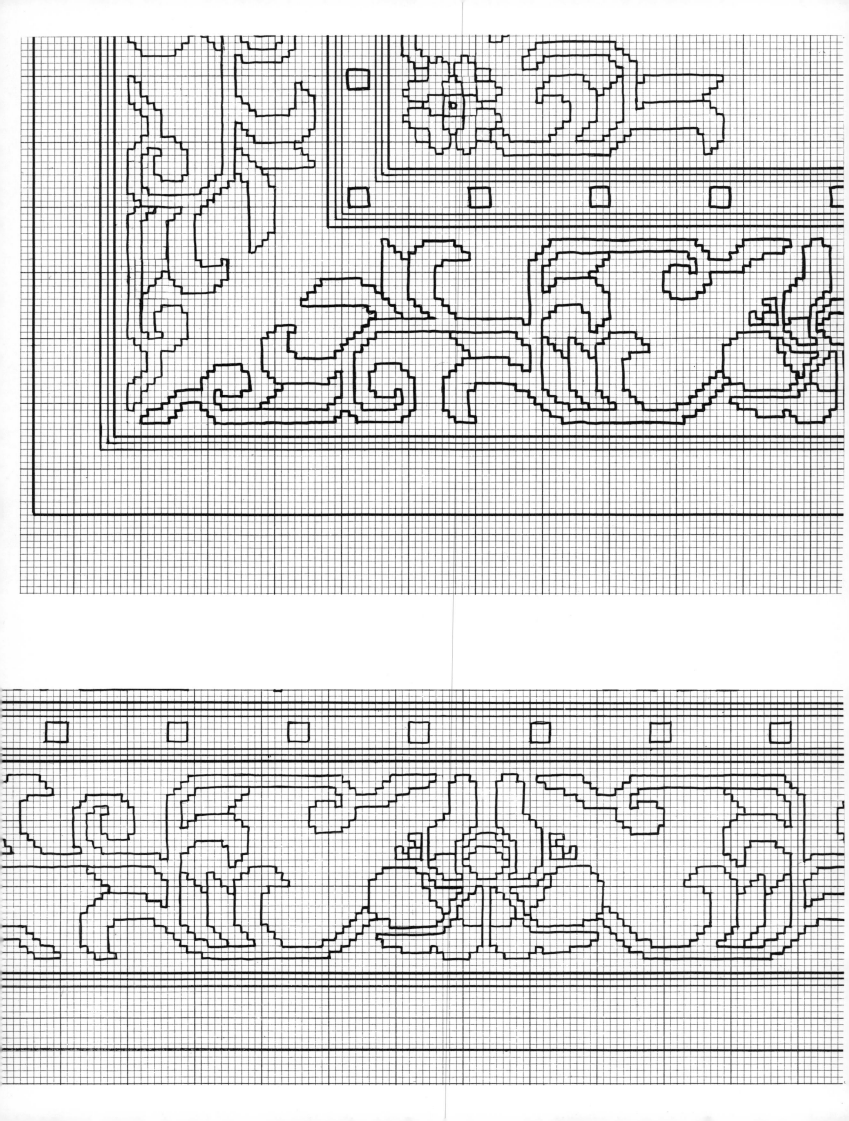

BOTTOM BORDER

SIDE BORDER

See pages 66–67 for complete rug

Garniture Rug

43″ x 60″

Worked on #8 Penelope canvas
Wool needed, see page xiii

This design was adapted from an Oriental rug, plate 62, in *Oriental Rugs in Colour*, by Preben Liebetrau, Macmillan, publishers.

The graph thread-count is 339 x 483. Bind off a piece of #8 Penelope canvas measuring 50″ x 66″. Mark center lines and outline work area. Mark graph lines in field. Do not mark graph lines in the border until you are ready to work the objects in each pictorial lozenge.

Four tones were used in the garniture rug. They are:

1. Nearly white
2. Light
3. Medium
4. Dark

The sample rug was made with Persian wool, using the full thread, all three strands. If you want a rug with a tight weave, add one extra strand of wool to the three-strand thread. You will then be working with four strands.

The key to the 9 colors used in the garniture rug follows:

1. 396 Palest blue
2. 395 Light blue
3. 386 Medium blue
4. 147 Palest amethyst
5. 137 Light amethyst
6. 127 Medium amethyst

63

7. 117 Dark amethyst
8. 553 Medium olive green
9. 512 Dark green

1. Work the objects in the field, using sample rug as a key to color and tonal value.
2. Work pearl border and key-fret border around field.
3. Fill in field.
4. Work dark bands around patterned border, and at each end of pictorial lozenges in patterned border.
5. Mark appropriate graph lines in each lozenge before you work the object in it.
6. Work background in lozenges.
7. Work patterned areas of border. Here I suggest that you mark the horizontal and vertical center threads of each patterned area. Then, by working outward from the intersections of these threads, your patterns will be properly centered.
8. Work dark border around the edge of the field.

Sample rug worked by Louise de Paoli.

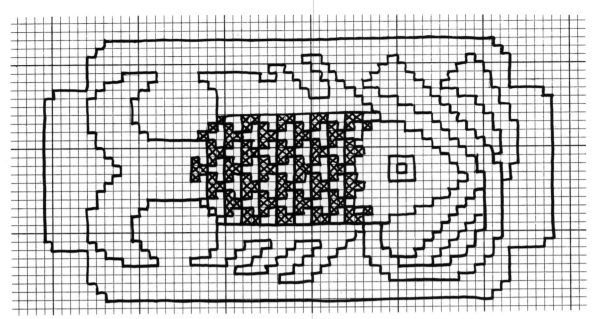

Designs for the border medallions (see pages 66 and 67) which
can be placed as you wish.

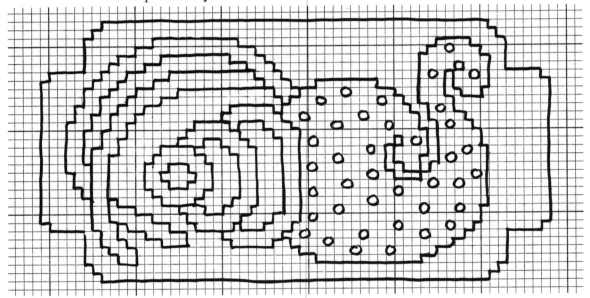

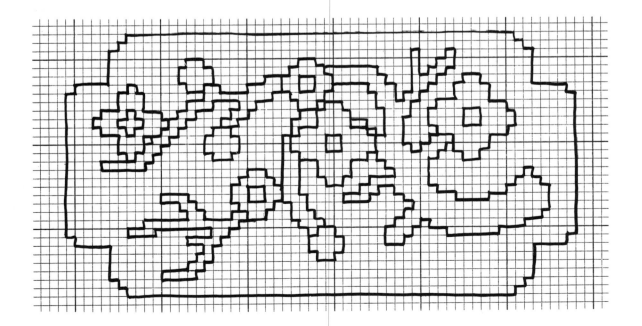

These designs could also be used for separate small pieces, such
as eyeglass cases or pincushions.

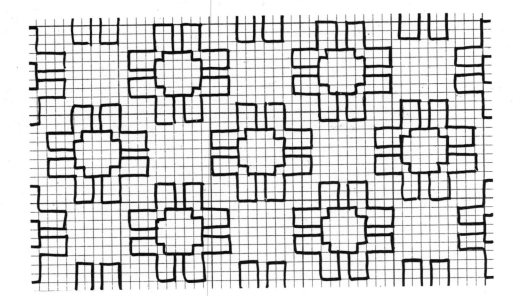

Graphs on pages 76-79 offer a selection of border designs to
to be used between the medallions (see pages 66 and 67).

These designs could be used as repeat patterns for any needle-point project.

Graphs on pages 76-79 offer a selection of border designs to
to be used between the medallions (see pages 66 and 67).

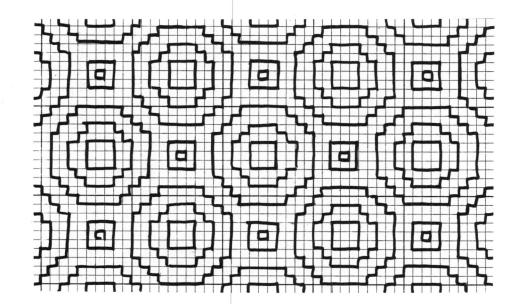

These designs could be used as repeat patterns for any needle-point project.

Fish Medallion Rug

54" x 78"

Worked on #8 Penelope canvas
Wool needed, see page xiii

The design for the center medallion in this rug was adapted from an antique Chinese bowl of the Yung Cheng period, 1723–1735.

The graph thread-count is 443 x 587. Bind off a piece of #8 Penelope canvas measuring 60" x 84". Mark center lines and outline work area. Mark graph lines for fish medallion. Do not mark graph lines in the border until you are ready to work the double cash motifs and eternal knots in their respective lozenges or corner panels.

Three tones are used in the Fish Medallion rug. They are:

1. White
2. Medium
3. Dark

The sample rug was made with Persian wool, using the full thread, all three strands. If you want a rug with a tight weave, add one extra strand of wool to the three-strand thread. You will then be working with four strands.

NOTE: The field around the medallion was worked in the brick stitch. Use five or six strands of wool, whichever you find covers the canvas to your satisfaction.

The key to the colors used in the sample rug follows:

1. 010 Off-white
2. 952 Chinese lacquer red
   (available on special order)
3. 305 Navy

1. Using tones #1 and #3, work fish and trailing seaweed in center medallion.
2. Using tone #1, work border of incurling waves with scalloped outline. Also work the scalloped line around it.
3. Using tone #2, fill in background of fish medallion.
4. Work pearl border.
5. Work key-fret border.
6. Using tone #2, and the brick stitch, work background of field.
7. Using tone #2, work outlines of key-fret border and work outlines of lozenges and corner panels.
8. Using tones #2 and #3, work double cash motifs in border lozenges.
9. Using tone #3, work eternal knots in the four corner panels.
10. Using tone #2, work diaper pattern of swastika key fret in border.
11. Using tone #1, fill in border.
12. Using tone #2, work outer border.

Sample rug worked by Maggie Lane, Paul Griffith, and Charles Blackburn.

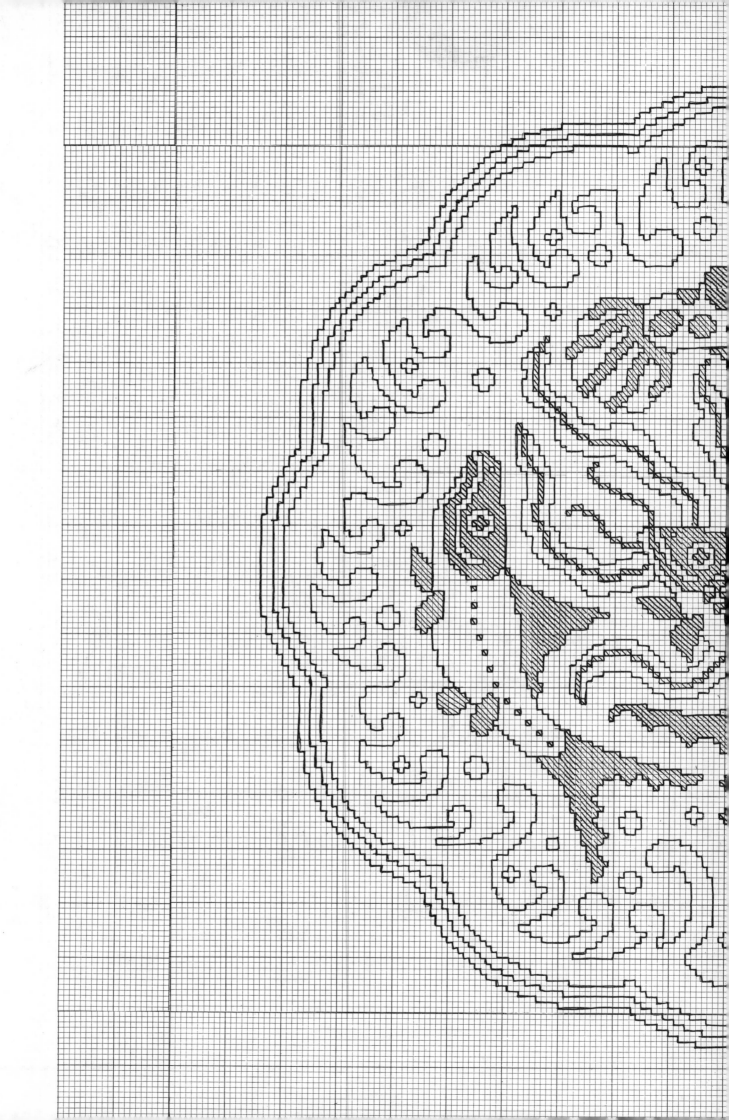

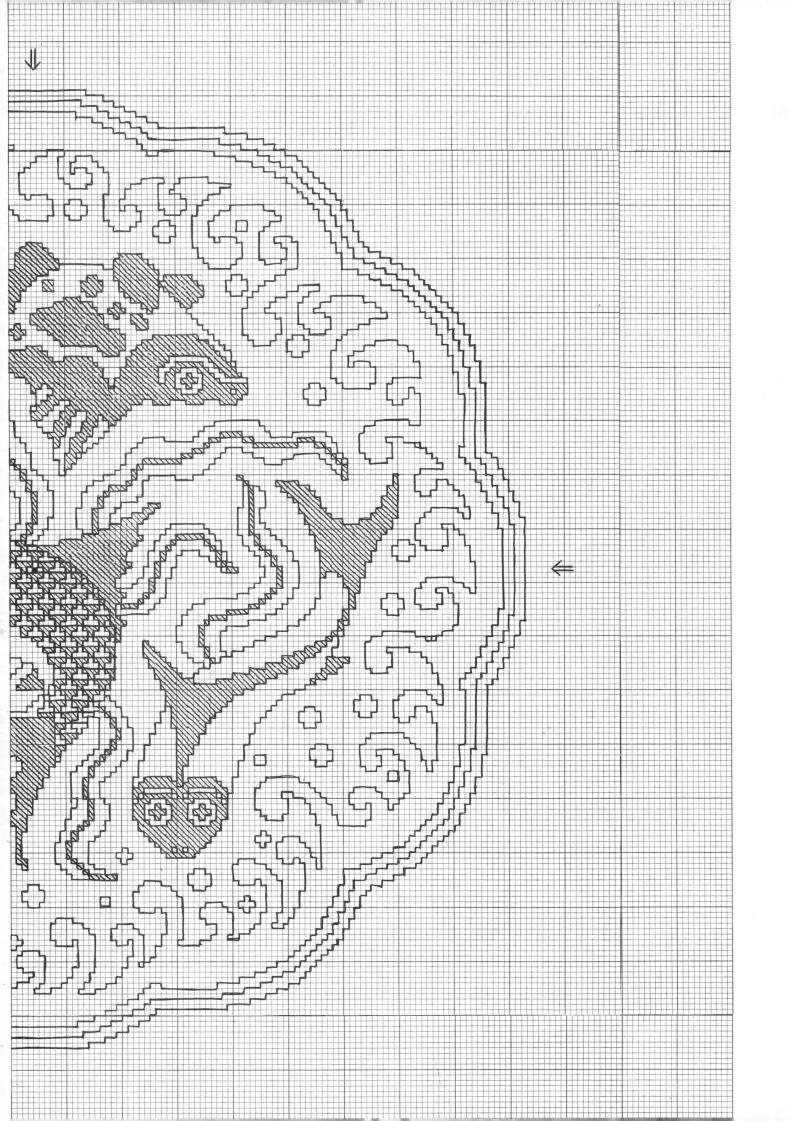

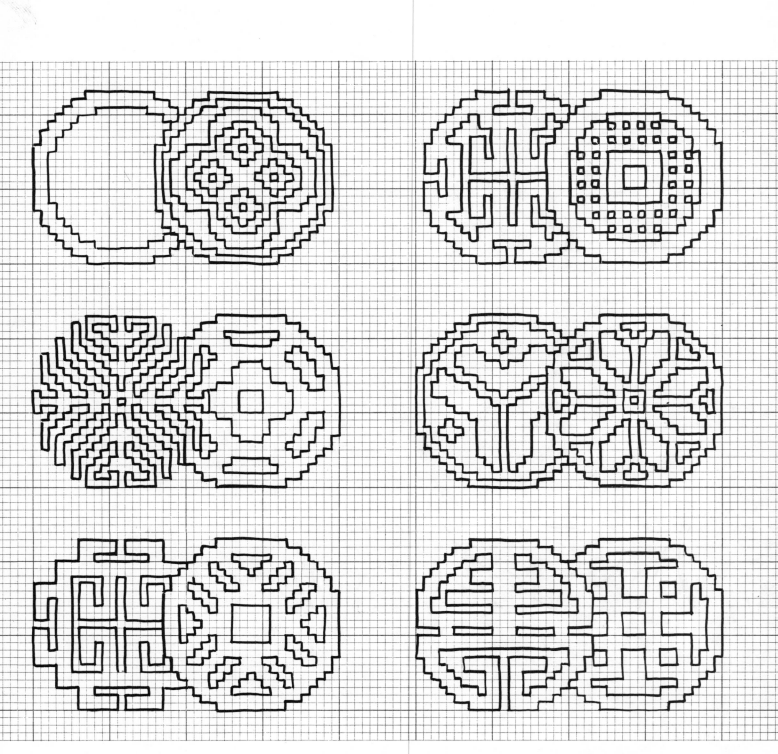

These are the coins for the lozenges in the border of the Fish Medallion rug. The upper two are for the upper side. The second two are for the lower side. The bottom two, tipped sidewise, are for the left and right sides. The one on the left leaves a blank in which you may insert your initials.

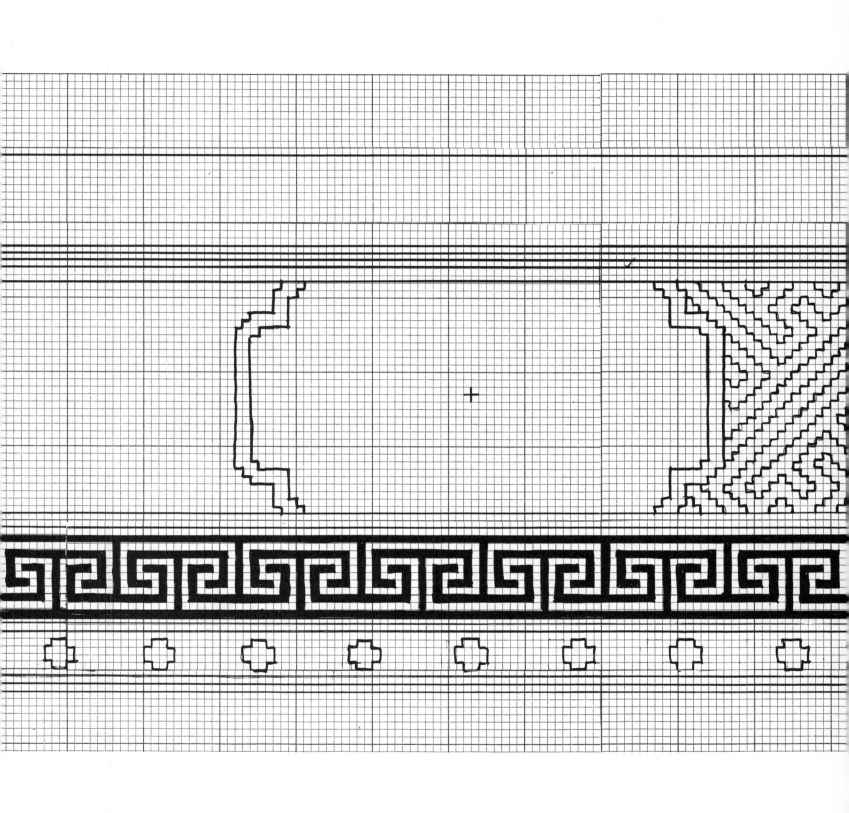

Flying Cranes Rug

36″ x 59″

Worked on #10 mono canvas
Wool needed, see page xiii

This design was adapted from an 18th-century Chinese rug at the Textile Museum, Washington, D.C.

The graph thread-count is 557 x 339. Bind off a piece of #10 mono canvas measuring 42″ x 65″. Mark center lines and outline work area. Mark graph lines in the field. When marking graph lines in the field, mark one half only, up to and including center motif. Turn canvas and graph and mark second half of field only up to center motif. (In this half you could use a second color marking pen to avoid confusion.) You should not find them necessary for working the borders.

Four tones are used in the Flying Cranes rug. They are:

1. White
2. Light
3. Medium dark
4. Dark

The sample rug was made with Persian wool, using the full thread, all three strands.

The key to the colors used in the sample rug follows:

1. 010 Off-white
2. 563 Celadon
3. 145 Brown
4. 105 Tête de Nègre

1. Using tone #2, work happiness character and scalloped border of central motif. Fill in with tone #1.

2. Using tone #2, work detail lines in flying cranes. Finish cranes with tone #1.
3. Using tone #4, outline field, then work interlocking coin pattern in field.
4. Using tone #3, fill in background of field.
5. Using tone #3, work the two 2-row bands outlining swastika border.
6. Using tone #2, work swastika key fret, then fill in with tone #1.
7. Using tone #1, work two row band next to outer border.
8. Using tones #1, #2, #3, and #4, work zigzag border.
9. Using tone #4, work outer border.

Sample rug worked by Maggie Lane and Barbara Rubinstein.

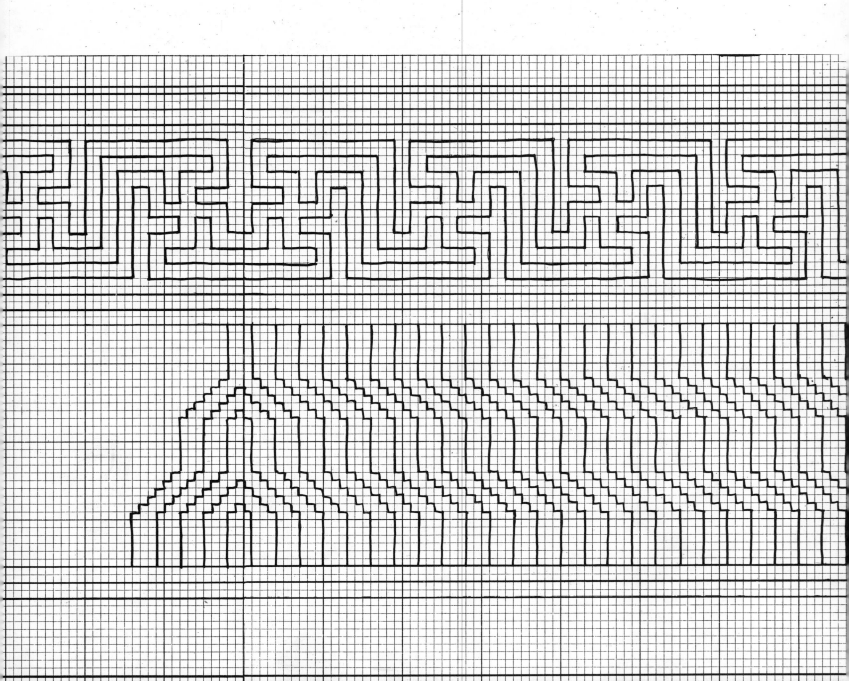

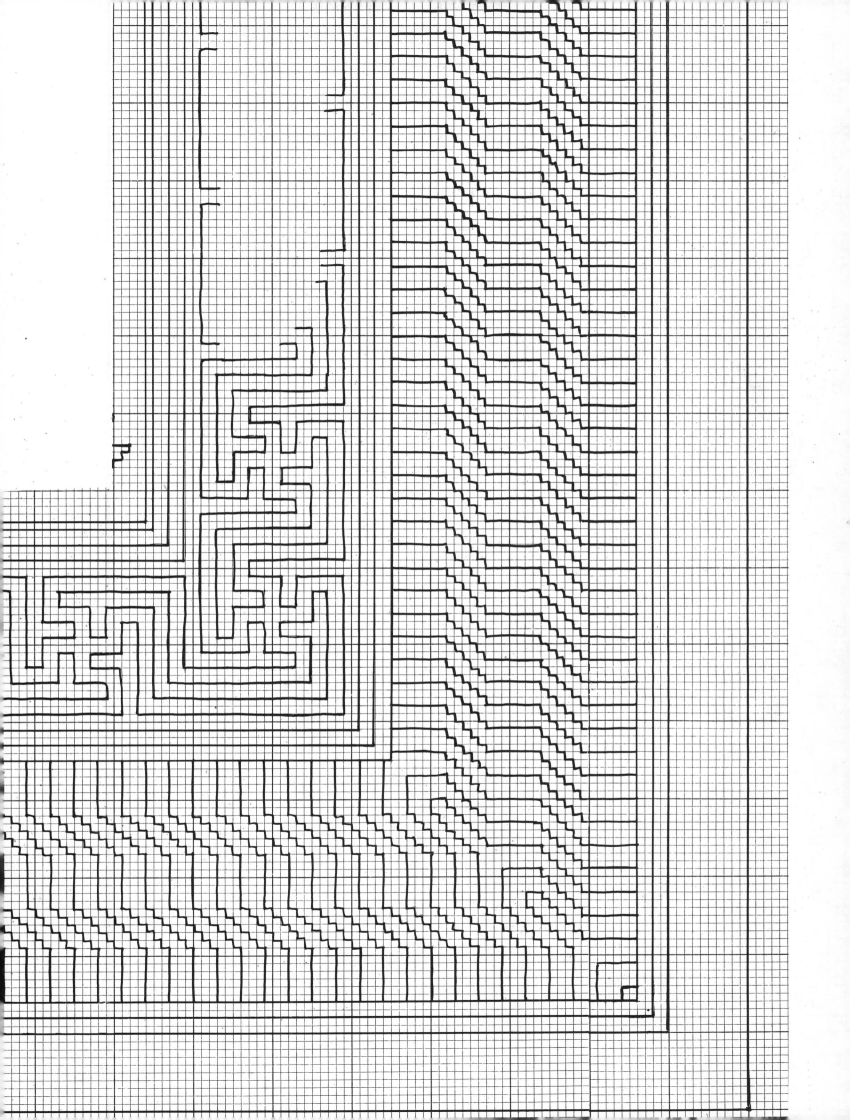

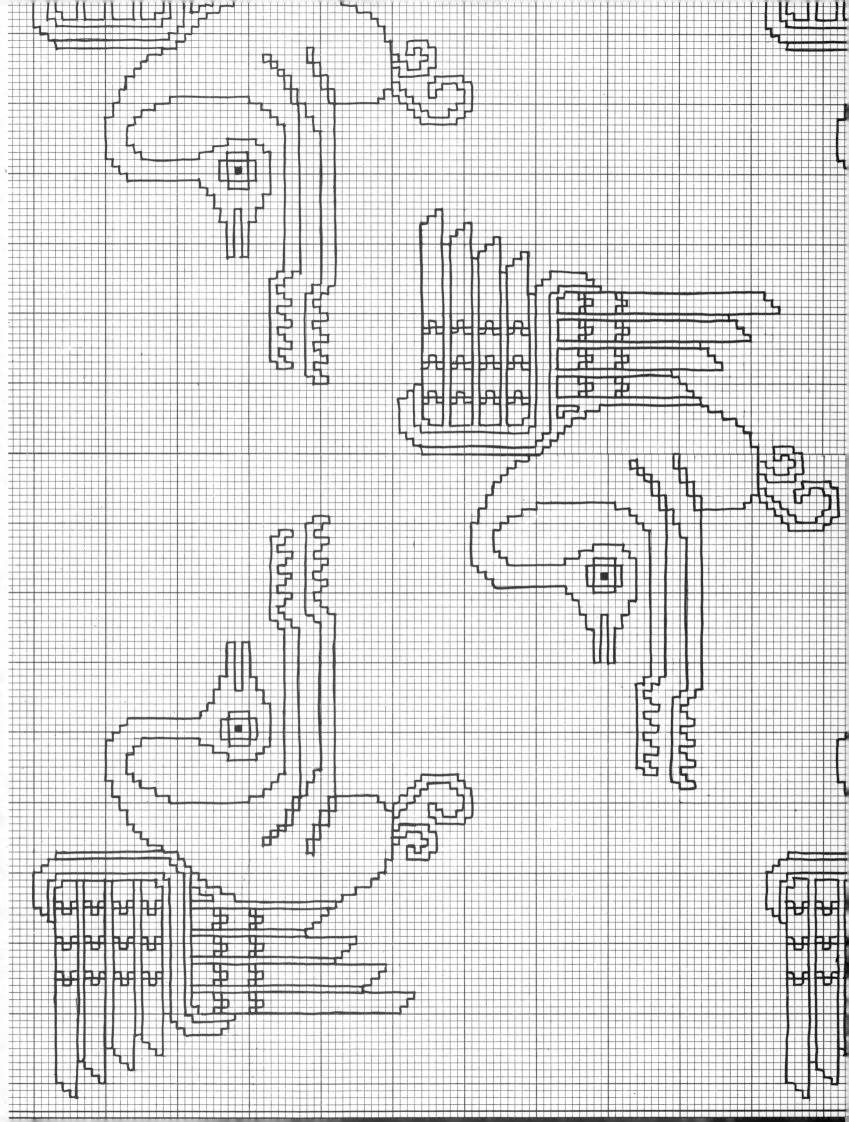

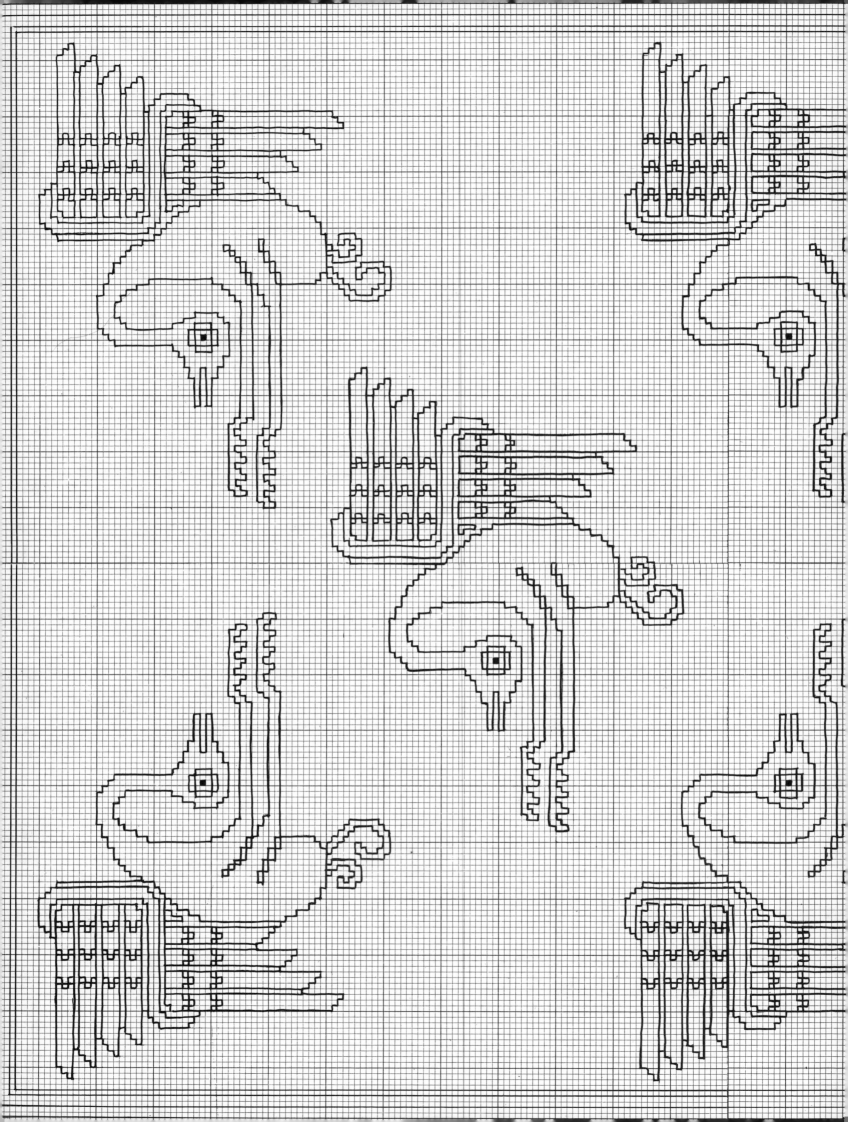

Elephant Panel

30″ x 72″

Worked on #10 mono canvas
Wool needed, see page xiii

This design was adapted from an elephant embroidered on a hanging belonging to the Metropolitan Museum of Art, New York City. The upper and lower parts of the panel were adapted from an antique Chinese pillar rug.

The design has three parts. The graph thread-count is 301 x 172 for the upper, or tassel section, 301 x 301 for the center section, or elephant square, 301 x 179 for the lower, or waves section. The total thread count is 301 x 652.

Bind off a piece of #10 mono canvas measuring 36″ x 78″. Mark vertical center line. Mark horizontal center line in the middle of the elephant square. Outline work area. Mark graph lines. NOTE 1: When working this design you may wish to lower the outer dark clouds above the elephant. I would suggest lowering them so that the upper edge of each cloud is level with the bottom edge of the other two more central clouds directly above the elephant. NOTE 2: You can make this panel into a horizontal rug by working the wave borders at both sides of the elephant, as shown (see sketch):

The sample panel was made with Persian wool, using the full threads, all three strands.

NOTE: When working the tassels at the top of the hanging, work the vertical rows of lighter color in the continental stitch with the stitches slanting in the same direction as all other stitches in the rug. When working the vertical rows of the darker color, however, work them also in the continental stitch, *but slant the stitches in the opposite direction to all other stitches in the rug.* (Do this by turning your work sidewise.) This will eliminate any distortion of the canvas caused by the use of repeated rows of continental stitch all pulling in the same direction.

Twenty tones and colors were used in the Elephant Panel. The key follows:

1. 005 White
2. 010 Off-white
3. 015 Ivory white
4. 541 Pale straw
5. 462 Fawn tan
6. 427 Pumpkin yellow
7. 440 Saffron yellow (background color)
8. 032 Pale blue
9. 382 Light blue
10. 381 Medium blue
11. 330 Medium dark blue
12. 365 Navy blue
13. 593 Pale olive green
14. 553 Medium olive green
15. 540 Dark olive green
16. 434 Medium orange
17. 424 Dark orange
18. 441 Light yellow
19. 447 Yellow
20. 210 Brick red

For the upper section—the key fret and tassels—the following colors were used:

1. 010 White key fret against 440 saffron yellow background
2. 010 White dots against 365 navy band
3. 365 Navy band above key fret
4. 010 White and 365 navy elephant heads and dotted connections
5. 365 Navy and 381 pale blue tassels with 541 straw tops
6. 015 Ivory and 541 straw tassels with 365 navy tops
7. 010 White outlines for clouds
8. 365 Navy and 424 dark orange inside clouds
9. 440 Saffron yellow background

For the middle section—the elephant—the following colors were used, starting from the top:

1. 541 Pale straw tracery
2. 015 Ivory flower, 210 red heart
3. 365 Navy knive and fork
4. 541 Pale straw supports for two large ornaments
5. 015 Ivory ornaments with 010 white details
6. 365 Navy fluttering ribbons
7. 593, 553, 540 olive fruit
8. 434, 424, 210 orange-red fruit
9. 382, 330, 365 blue fruit

NOTE: Each piece of fruit has 010 white for its center.

1. 015 Ivory bowl with 462 tan outlines
2. 381 and 330 Blue, and 553 and 593 green in the decorative band across the bowl
3. 462 Tan outlines for elephant
4. 015 Elephant except for 001 white ears, tusks, toenails, and white of eyes
   Work the howdah and harness as you see fit.
5. 440 Saffron yellow background

For the lower section of clouds, spray, mountains, curling waves, and zigzag waves the following colors were used:

1. 010 White outlines for clouds, 365 navy inside clouds
2. 010 White spray above mountains
3. 010 White tops of mountains, outlines of curling waves underneath, and wherever white appears in zigzag waves below curling waves

Geometric mountains progress inward from 010 white outer line, to 365 navy, to 381 medium blue, to 427 pumpkin yellow, to 440 saffron yellow, to 015 ivory white—the largest or inner part of each mountain.

The insides of the curling wave band are 365 navy, 427 pumpkin yellow, and 440 saffron yellow.

Zigzag waves are: 365 navy, 381 medium blue, and 010 white . . . 427 pumpkin yellow, 447 yellow, and 010 white . . . 440 saffron yellow, 441 lighter yellow, and 010 white . . . *Repeat*.

Sample panel worked by Charles Blackburn.

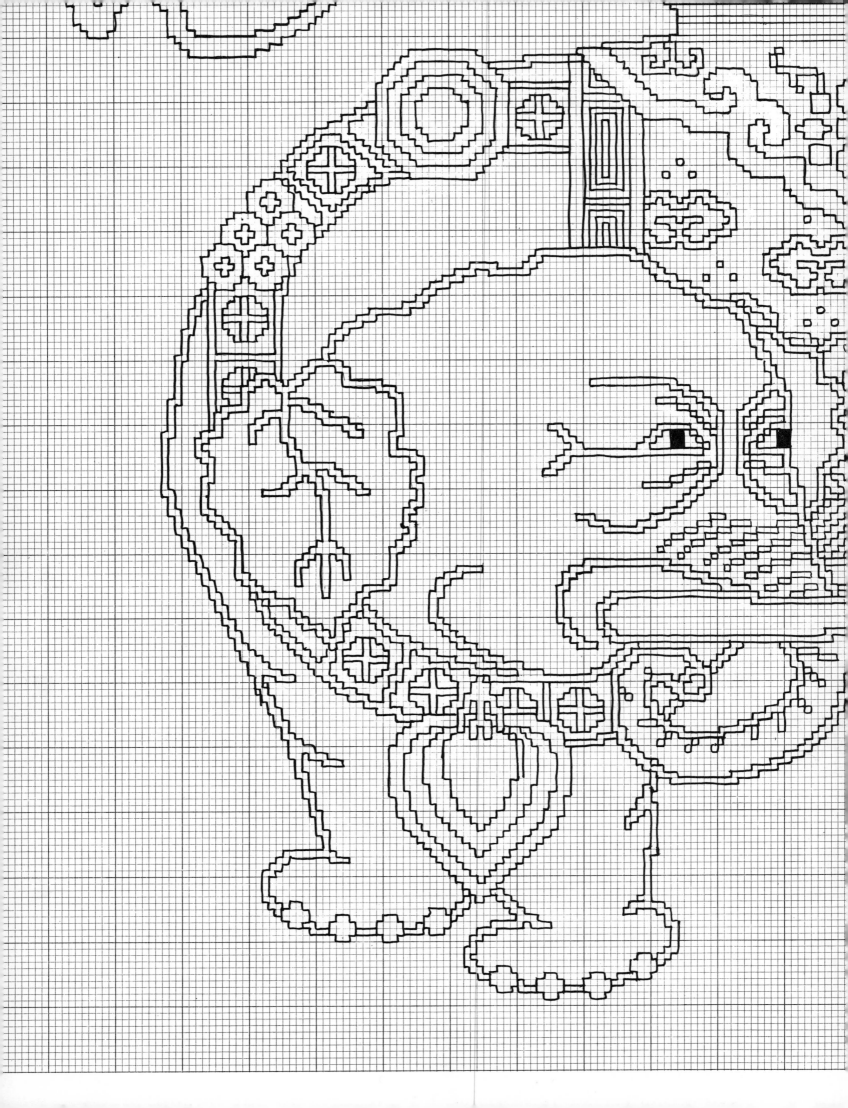

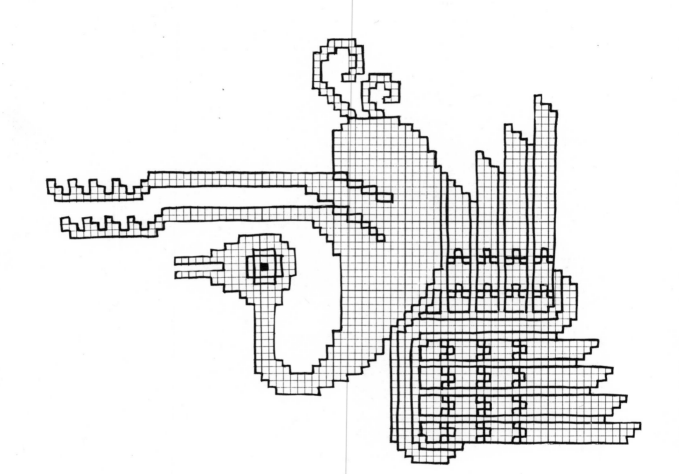

Bibliography

A View of Chinese Rugs
H. A. Lorentz, Routledge and Kegan Paul, Ltd., 1973.

Islamic Carpets
Joseph V. McMullen, Near Eastern Art Research Center, Inc.,
New York, 1965.

Oriental Rugs in Color
Preben Liebetrau, Macmillan, 1963.

A Connoisseur's Guide to Oriental Carpets
E. Gans-Ruedin, Charles E. Tuttle, 1971.

Oriental Rugs in the Metropolitan Museum of Art
M. S. Dimand and Jean Mailey, New York, The Metropolitan
Museum of Art, 1973.

Notes